JOURNEY THROUGH
KENYA

LIZ GOGERLY AND ROB HUNT

W

FRANKLIN WATTS

LONDON • SYDNEY

Franklin Watts
First published in Great Britain in paperback in 2018 by The Watts Publishing Group

Credits
Editor in Chief: John C. Miles
Series Editor: Amy Stephenson
Series Designer: Emma DeBanks
Picture Researcher: Diana Morris
Picture credits: American Spirit/Dreamstime: 6bc, 23. Ammonitefoto/Dreamstime: 26. Andreanit/Dreamstime: 17b. Andrew 7726/Dreamstime: 7tr. Antonella 865/Dreamstime: 10b. Aprescindere/Dreamstime: 21cb, 21b. Aquanaut4/Dreamstime: 27t. Marina Assarova/Dreamstime: 7tl. Parawat Isarangura Ng Ayudhay/Dreamstime: 7cl. D Bergeron/Dreamstime: 18. Richard Bindley/Alamy: 28b. Justin Black/Dreamstime: 7tc. Byelikova/Dreamstime: 6br, 27br, 29t, 29b. Oksana Byelikova/Shutterstock: 8t. Volodymyr Byrdyak/Dreamstime: front cover. Claire C Photography/Dreamstime: 4t. Rick Carey/Shutterstock: 28t. Christianze/Dreamstime: 6cl, 11t. Roland Colling/Dreamstime: 1. Derejeb/Dreamstime: 25t. Divehive/Dreamstime: 7br. Dwld777/Dreamstime: 7bcl. www,elsatrust.org: 22. Mary Evans PL: 15t. Valeriy Eviakhov/Dreamstime: 6cr. Iakov Filimonov/Dreamstime: 7lc, 7cb. Grantotufo/Dreamstime: 7clb, 16b. Robert Harding PL/Superstock: 27bl. Gillian Hardy/Dreamstime: 10c. Martin Harvey/Alamy: 6clb, 20b. Imagebroker/Superstock: 19t. Images & Stories/Alamy: 21t. Isselee/Dreamstime: 7lcb. Izanbar/Dreamstime: 3b. John Lambert/Tips/ agefotostock: 25b. Zute Lightfoot/Alamy: 5c. Lunamarina/Dreamstime: 7bcrb, 7brb. Robyn Mackenzie/Dreamstime: 7trb. Marsel82/Dreamstime: 7bl. Masr/Dreamstime: 9b. © Mobius: 14c. Jesper Mogensen/Dreamstime: 5t. Alessio Moiola/Dreamstime: 21ct. Alexander Mychko Dreamstime: 4b. Nadsdi/Dreamstime: 6c, 17t. Neilom/Dreamstime: 8b, 13t. Anna Omelchenko/Dreamstime: 14b. Alexander Peers/Dreamstime: 7bcr. Magdalena Pirnea/Dreamstime; 9c. Stuart G Porter/Shutterstock: 11b. Maryann Preisinger My Topshelf/Dreamstime: 7rcb. Aliaksei Putau/Dreamstime: 12b. Pisiti Rapitpunt/Dreamstime: 7ta. Sommai Sommai/Dreamstime: 7rc. Dietmar Temps/Dreamstime: 16t. Titovstudio/Dreamstime: 7crb. Tokarsky/Dreamstime: 6t, 9t. Morgen Trolle/Dreamstime: 15c. Ekaterina Tsepova/Dreamstime: 7c. Lucas Vallecillos/agefotostock/Superstock: 19b. Viktor1/Shutterstock:24br Valentyn Volkov/Shutterstock: 7cr. Joshua Wanyama/Dreamstime: 24bl. John Wollwerth/Dreamstime: 13b.

Dewey number: 914.1
ISBN: 978 1 4451 3688 2

Printed in Malaysia

Franklin Watts
An imprint of
Hachette Children's Group
Part of The Watts Publishing Group
Carmelite House
50 Victoria Embankment
London EC4Y 0DZ

An Hachette UK Company
www.hachette.co.uk

www.franklinwatts.co.uk

CONTENTS

WELCOME TO KENYA!

Kuwakaribisha kwa Kenya! Welcome to Kenya! This fascinating country in East Africa combines the traditional with the modern. The country is diverse in every possible sense – it has a vast amount of wildlife; a hugely contrasting climate (wet and tropical on the coast, but very dry inland); and a wide variety of cultures, languages and religion.

Africa's melting pot

Officially called the Republic of Kenya, the birth of this relatively young country, resulted from the 'Scramble for Africa' in the late 19th century, when European powers divided up East Africa between them, paying little attention to the wishes of the tribal people who lived there. The British government formed the British East African Protectorate in 1895, which became the crown colony of Kenya in 1920. In the early 20th century, British settlers arrived. Since then, people of many nationalities have moved to Kenya, which has one of the most diverse populations in Africa.

Over 60 languages are spoken in Kenya, but the main languages are Swahili and English. Swahili is strongly influenced by Arabic, but uses words borrowed from English, German, Portuguese, Hindustani and French.

▲ The busy city of Nairobi

Merits of mixing

Kenya's diversity can sometimes lead to tension, but tension can also bring creativity. A good example is the popular music genre, *genge*. This mixture of hip hop and traditional African sounds is often sung in a slang version of Swahili called 'Sheng'. Another example is the fusion cuisine you will encounter. Indian and Kenyan cooking styles mixed together produce some truly exotic dishes.

► A Kenyan-Indian chicken curry.

► Part of the Great Rift Valley runs through Kenya, from Lake Turkana in the north to the Tanzanian border in the south.

Cradle of humanity

There is widely accepted evidence to suggest that Kenya and the surrounding area is the birthplace of humanity. Fossils of our earliest ancestors – known as hominids – have been found in the Great Rift Valley, and Kenya boasts the largest number of these fossils, with the oldest dating back 7 million years.

Getting around

Public transport around Kenya is quite limited. Locals travel in privately owned minibuses called *matutus* (see right). They are easy to spot because they are highly decorated and play loud music to attract customers. On your journey you will travel mainly by hired car and private plane, as boats, trains and scheduled flights serve only a limited number of destinations.

Bumpy landings

Flying by private plane is an exciting way to see this huge country. Not only will you be able to see the varied landscapes below you, you'll experience taking off and landing at some of the unusual airstrips dotted around Kenya. Some have tarmac, but many are just strips of grass, soil or sand, so be prepared for some bumpy landings!

Trouble in paradise

Malaria is the biggest threat to human life in Kenya. In 2012, 30,000 Kenyans died from the disease and in the same year one in every 20 deaths worldwide from malaria was in Kenya. This deadly illness is spread by mosquitoes — mainly during the rainy season — and it is worse at lower altitudes, around Lake Victoria and in coastal regions. Kenyans have to live with the constant risk of contracting malaria, but many do not have the money to pay for mosquito drugs or nets.

To help prevent malaria on your travels, you should always take protective medicine, use insect repellent and sleep under a mosquito net.

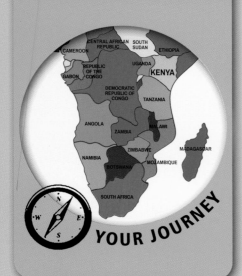

YOUR JOURNEY

JOURNEY PLANNER

1

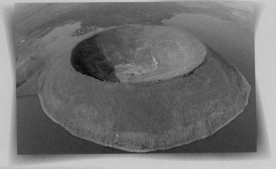

2

3

Lake Vic

4

6

KEY

——————	**your route around Kenya**
- - - - - - -	**flight / ferry**
——————	**river**
——————	**road**
★	**capital city**

5

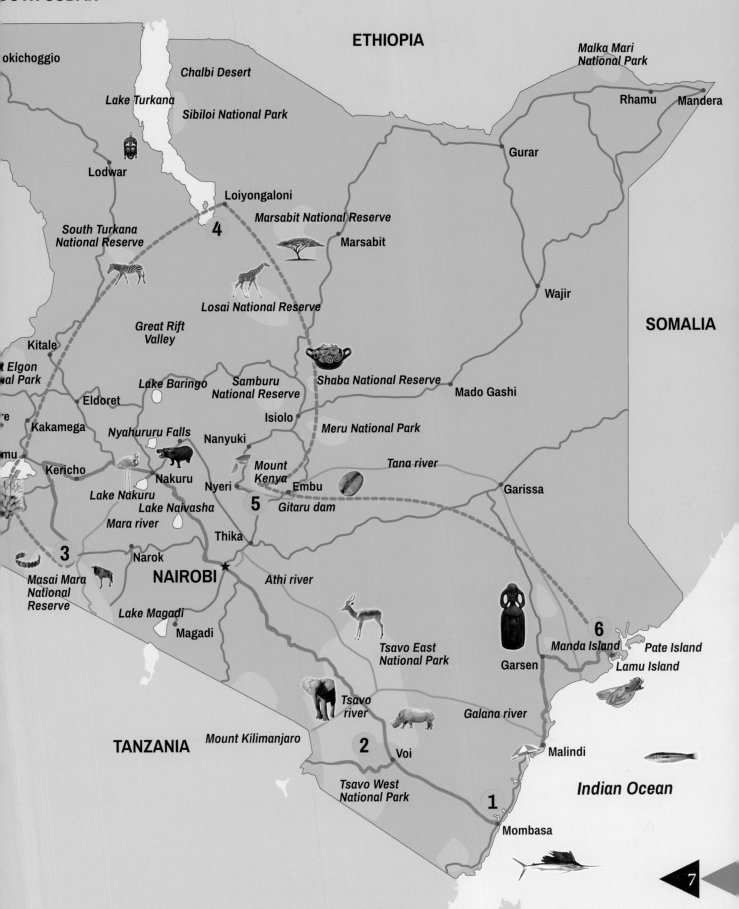

SOUTH SUDAN

ETHIOPIA

okichoggio

Malka Mari National Park

Chalbi Desert

Lake Turkana

Sibiloi National Park

Rhamu   Mandera

Lodwar

Loiyongaloni

Gurar

South Turkana National Reserve

4

Marsabit National Reserve

Marsabit

SOMALIA

Losai National Reserve

Wajir

Kitale

Great Rift Valley

t Elgon
al Park

Eldoret

Lake Baringo

Samburu National Reserve

Shaba National Reserve

Mado Gashi

Kakamega

Nyahururu Falls

Nanyuki

Isiolo

Meru National Park

Tana river

Kericho

Nakuru

Nyeri

Mount Kenya

Embu

Garissa

Lake Nakuru

Lake Naivasha

5

Gitaru dam

Mara river

Thika

3

Narok

NAIROBI

Athi river

Masai Mara National Reserve

Lake Magadi

Magadi

6

Manda Island   *Pate Island*

Garsen

Lamu Island

TANZANIA

Mount Kilimanjaro

Tsavo East National Park

Tsavo river

Galana river

Malindi

Indian Ocean

2

Voi

Tsavo West National Park

1

Mombasa

7

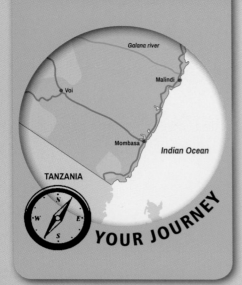

YOUR JOURNEY

MOMBASA

You start your journey around Kenya in the coastal city of Mombasa. As your plane lands at Moi International Airport, prepare for a blast of tropical heat. The Equator crosses Kenya and the average temperature all year round in Mombasa is 30 degrees Celsius.

▲ Mombasa is surrounded by many small harbours.

▲ One of the most exhilarating ways to get around Mombasa is by *tuk tuk* – a three-wheeled taxi.

Island in the sun

Mombasa is the second-largest city in Kenya, with a population of around 1.3 million. Mombasa has a long history of international trade, which is down to its naturally deep harbour. It is East Africa's largest port and it trades in goods such as cement and oil. The city is actually on an island in the Indian Ocean, and is separated from the mainland by two creeks. Bridges connect the north and east of the city to the mainland, whereas from the south of the city you'll need to jump aboard a ferry.

Spice of life

You're certain of a warm welcome in this bustling, cosmopolitan and multicultural city. This is the homeland of the Swahili people of East Africa. They speak Swahili and follow a strict Islamic code. There are many other Kenyan ethnic groups here. Communities from Portugal, Iran, India, Britain and Somalia have settled here and the city's rich heritage is reflected in its delicious array of food. For breakfast try *maharagwe*: a local dish that combines beans and coconut.

▲ The Old Town is one of the best places to experience Mombasa's cultural diversity.

Indian Ocean paradise

Mombasa is Kenya's number one tourist destination, mostly due to its beautiful tropical beaches. White powdery sands and palm trees await you on the north and south coasts. The clear blue waters are perfect for swimming and snorkelling. Real beach lovers can head to Diani Beach, about half an hour south of Mombasa. This long, sandy beach is rated one of the most beautiful beaches in the world. After a day there you can listen or dance to some of Kenya's best new music at the relaxed beach cafes.

▲ Fort Jesus was built to defend the port of Mombasa from attack.

Fort Jesus

The most popular historic site in Mombasa is Fort Jesus. The fort was begun by the Portuguese in 1593 and is now a UNESCO World Heritage Site. It's a great place to discover Mombasa's history and learn about the struggle for power in Mombasa between the local people, the Portuguese, the Arabs, and the British.

▲ Tourists can take a camel ride along the pristine sands of Diani Beach.

TSAVO

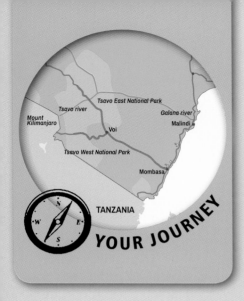

YOUR JOURNEY

Say the word 'Africa' and most people think about the stunning wildlife. Africa has areas of wilderness where wild animals like lions, elephants, zebra and rhinos roam. Kenya is one of the best places to go on safari, which is a key contributor to Kenya's biggest industry – tourism. In the Tsavo National Parks you will feel that your real African adventure has begun ...

▼ A herd of elephants walk across the dry, red earth of the Tsavo.

Hit the road

If you want to go on a wild safari then you will need a 4x4 vehicle like a Land Rover or Land Cruiser with a driver/safari guide. Take the main highway from Mombasa to Nairobi to get to Tsavo. It is safer to make the journey in these big vehicles, especially when you discover the road is full of potholes and that parts of it disappear during the rainy season. In about 3 hours you'll hit the dusty red roads that cover the final distance to Tsavo.

▲ Safari vehicles on the road to Tsavo.

Tsavo East and West

Tsavo has two national parks, Tsavo East and Tsavo West, which together form one of the largest areas of national park in the world, and cover four per cent of Kenya's land area. Tsavo East is flatter and drier with vast scrubland plains. If you want to avoid tourists, this is the park for you. On a hot day, head to Lugard's Falls on the Galana river. Sit back and admire the rapids as they crash against the beautiful pink, grey and white rocks, but watch out for crocodiles – they are everywhere!

You'll see big game animals in both parks, but Tsavo West is more popular with tourists due to its more varied landscape and views of Mount Kilimanjaro – Africa's highest mountain (5,895 m) – which lies just over the border in Tanzania.

▲ A male Tsavo lion.

Tsavo lions

On your safari, you may be lucky enough to spot a Tsavo lion. The males are bigger than most other types of lion and take an active part in hunting. Hopefully, you won't encounter a man-eating Tsavo lion as the workers on the Kenya-Uganda Railway (see page 12) did in 1898. A pair of male lions stalked and killed about 135 victims in just one year!

Ivory trade

Tsavo is home to some of the largest herds of elephants in Kenya. Sadly, in the 1970s and 1980s about 80 per cent of the elephants in Tsavo were killed by poachers. Numbers fell from 35,000 to 6,500 by the late 1980s. However, today the poachers are still killing elephants for their valuable ivory tusks. Sadly, one of Africa's other beautiful animals, the rhino, is also targeted for its horns. Ivory and horns are big business as demand in China continues to drive the market.

▲ Rhinos are likely to become extinct if the demand for their horns continues.

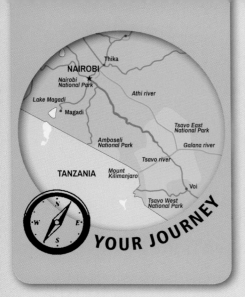

YOUR JOURNEY

NAIROBI

Leave Tsavo behind and take a train to to Kenya's capital city, Nairobi. The biggest city in Kenya has two nicknames – 'the Green City in the Sun' and, because of the crime rate, 'Nairobbery'. As both names suggest, you can enjoy the highs and lows of rural and urban life in this relatively new city.

Lunatic Line

Three times a week a passenger train travels between Mombasa and Nairobi. The Kenya-Uganda Railway was built between 1895 and 1901 by British colonists and everything about the trip is like stepping back in time, from the railway stations to the faded luxury of the railway carriages. It was nicknamed the 'Lunatic Line' due to the amount of money it cost to build, the number of workers who died building it and the rather rickety trains. It can take 24 hours on the train, so most Kenyans prefer to drive or take a 1 hour flight to Nairobi, but you won't get the same sense of drama and adventure!

Maasai land

Nairobi gets its name from the Maasai people (see page 16) who lived in the area before British settlers arrived in the late 19th century. The Maasai called a local water hole *enkare nyrobi,* which translates as 'cool water' and in fact the whole area was once swampland. Nairobi became the headquarters of the British-owned Uganda Railway Company in 1899 and the city has been expanding ever since.

▼ An old diesel train on the 'Lunatic Line'.

▶ A Maasai market in Nairobi held outside the old courthouse building.

Colonialism in Kenya

In 1895 the British took control of what is now Kenya (see page 4) and called the area the East African Protectorate. By 1905 Nairobi had become the capital. As you walk around Nairobi today you can still see evidence of its colonial past, including government buildings, such as City Hall, its museums, hotels, libraries and cathedrals.

Kenyan independence

In 1963 Kenya gained independence from Britain and Jomo Kenyatta (1891–1978) became Kenya's first independent leader. Nairobi is thriving as Kenya's financial and ICT centre and today it is a modern city with a population of about 3.1 million. Skyscrapers have shot up and house some of Africa's biggest businesses, and international companies like Google, Coca Cola and Mitsubishi Motors.

City park

Nairobi is an incredibly leafy city with trees, parks and arboretums. Nairobi National Park lies within the city boundary and it was Kenya's first national park. Most of this small park is open grass plains and is home to wildlife including lions, hippos and hyenas.

▼ A giraffe roams in Nairobi National Park with Nairobi's skyscrapers in the background.

Money in 'mitumba'

Mitumba is a Swahili word that means 'bundles of second-hand clothes'. These clothes come from the UK and other Western countries, and are sold in markets all over Africa. Mitumba is big business in Nairobi, and Gikomba is the largest mitumba market in the city with an estimated 65,000 workers.

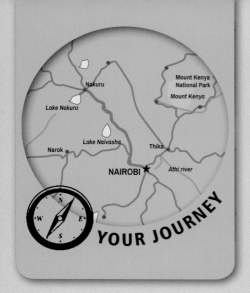

NAIROBI TO NAKURU

From Nairobi it's about a 160-km drive to Lake Nakuru, a soda lake where you'll see flocks of flamingoes that appear to turn the water pink. En route, stop off at Lake Naivasha to see water buffalo and hundreds of hippos.

Africa's cheapest car

If you want to drive a car made in Africa and designed especially for Africa's rough roads, then hire a Mobius II. This tough new car was launched in October 2014 and it is cheap because it doesn't have expensive extras like air con or even windows.

Manufactured in Nairobi, the car was the idea of a young British entrepreneur called Joel Jackson. "Mobius has the chance to change the transport network in Africa," says Jackson. This means that local farmers now have the means to transport their goods more easily over difficult terrain.

▲ The 'no frills' Mobius II.

Lake Naivasha

Lake Naivasha lies within the Great Rift Valley, a vast geographical feature that formed when two tectonic plates pulled apart. The valley runs roughly north to south through Kenya, and is part of a fault system that runs 6,000 km from the Middle East to East Africa.

From the road you will have majestic views across the Great Rift Valley before you reach the vast freshwater Lake Naivasha. The lake is the highest of all the Rift Valley lakes at 1,884 m above sea level. It's about 13 km across and is home to hippos, waterbuck and water buffalo. If you're feeling brave, take a boat trip to enjoy the lake's beauty and see the wildlife.

▶ Lady Idina Sackville was one of the Happy Valley Set.

Happy Valley Set

Step back in time to the 1920s and 1930s and you may have encountered a group of wealthy white people around the shores of Lake Naivasha. The 'Happy Valley Set', as they became known, were mostly of British origin and were famous for their lavish lifestyle and scandalous behaviour.

▲ Hippos are the most dangerous land animal in Africa. Highly territorial, hippos are aggressive both on land and in water!

Lake Nakuru

You will have to tear yourself away from the peace and beauty of Lake Naivasha and drive on to Lake Nakuru. Just over an hour away by car, it is the highest soda lake in the area. Its warm, shallow waters are mainly alkaline with a high mineral content, which means algae grow well here. Lake Nakuru has been a national park since 1968 and is famous for its flamingoes, which feed on the algae.

▼ Pink flamingoes feeding in Lake Nakuru.

YOUR JOURNEY

LAND OF THE MASAI MARA

Get on the road again and head west of the Great Rift Valley to the Masai Mara National Reserve. This is another top destination for wildlife, but you'll also be able to meet and discover more about the Maasai people.

The Maasai

The Maasai of Kenya and Tanzania are a semi-nomadic people who have lived on the dry plains of East Africa for hundreds of years. They are easily recognisable by the bright red *shuka* cloth they wear and their colourful beaded jewellery.

The Maasai are subsistence farmers who survive mostly from raising cattle (they eat the meat, drink the milk and even drink the blood when they are ill or after childbirth). The wealth of a Maasai warrior is still determined by how many cattle and children he has. If you're lucky you may see Maasai warriors singing and performing their traditional jumping dance (see above, right). You may also pick up a few words in Maa, the language of the Maasai.

▶ Every piece of Maasai beaded jewellery is unique.

Meaning in the beads

Maasai jewellery is made by Maasai women from clay, bone, copper and brass. The beadwork is full of meaning; for example red stands for bravery, unity and blood. Yellow and orange mean hospitality, and green signifies the land and health.

◀ Floating above the Masai Mara in a hot-air balloon is a unique way to travel. As it is so quiet, it also means you are less likely to disturb the wildlife below.

The National Reserve

The Masai Mara National Reserve is named after the local Maasai people and the Mara river, which flows through the region. In the local Maa language, *Mara* means 'spotted'. When you reach the grassy plains of the Masai Mara, you'll see the landscape is 'spotted' or dotted with acacia trees, shrubs and patches of scrub. The Masai Mara lies at 1,500 m above sea level, so there is abundant rainfall and a slightly milder climate than lower regions, which make this the perfect location for wildlife to thrive.

Wilderness in danger

Kenya's economy needs tourism, but the tourism industry is also threatening to ruin the Masai Mara forever. More luxury hotels and safari lodges are being built, which means the animal habitat is disappearing. One day this may spell the end of the animals and traditional Maasai way of life.

▶ Thousands of wildebeest cross the Mara river during their annual migration.

The greatest migration on Earth

If you arrive in the National Reserve between July and October, you may witness the great wildebeest migration. Each year more than a million wildebeest and zebra travel from Tanzania and cross the Mara river into the Masai Mara. This is nature at its most dramatic, as the animals try to cross the river without being trampled or snapped up by crocodiles. One of the best ways to see it all is from above, in a hot-air balloon. Lots of companies fly balloon safaris in the area, so take your pick!

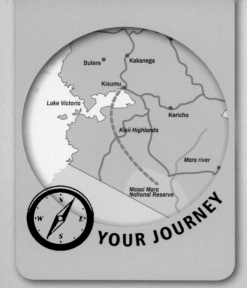

YOUR JOURNEY

LAKE VICTORIA

Lake Victoria is the second largest freshwater lake in the world and it is your next destination. Climb aboard a light aircraft at Mara Serena airstrip and you'll be there in less than an hour. Look down as you fly over the Kisii Highlands. This is one of Kenya's most fertile agricultural areas where a variety of crops are grown, including bananas, maize and pineapples.

Africa's largest lake

Lake Victoria is Africa's largest lake. Its surface area of 68,800 square km is more than three times the size of Wales! Three countries border it – Uganda, Kenya and Tanzania. This massive tropical lake is actually quite shallow with average depths of around 40 m. It is believed to be over 400,000 years old but it wasn't 'discovered' by a European – the British explorer John Hanning Speke (1827–1864) – until 1858. He named it after the British monarch, Queen Victoria (1819–1901).

Fish supper

If you want to savour the beauty of the lake and its surroundings, take a boat trip. Fishing is another popular activity for tourists, especially if you can net yourself a Nile perch or tilapia for supper. However, it's worth remembering that many of the local people are so poor they can't afford to eat whole fish – instead they eat what is known as *umgogowazi*, which is basically the fish heads, tails and guts. Also, overfishing is contributing to declining fish stocks and less wildlife in and around this great lake.

▲ Tilapia fish outside a restaurant on the banks of Lake Victoria.

Keep out of the water

Lake Victoria may look spectacular but don't be tempted to go swimming. A tiny parasitic worm that lives in the water can make you really ill with an infection called bilharzia. If left untreated, bilharzia can lead to some nasty symptoms later in life. These include coughing up blood and seizures.

▼ Children and a fisherman rest inside fishing boats on the shore of Lake Victoria.

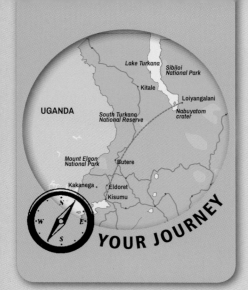

YOUR JOURNEY

TURKANA BASIN

It may feel that your journey around Kenya has mainly been hopping from one lake to another, but these lakes are an important source of water in this hot country. Next you're off to another lake in Kenya's Great Rift Valley – Lake Turkana. It is in the north of Kenya and its northern banks are actually in the neighbouring country of Ethiopia.

The Jade Sea

The best way to get to Lake Turkana – also known as the Jade Sea – is by chartered plane from Kisumu Airport. If you're feeling adventurous you could travel by road but it will take a long time and the going gets tough in the heat. Much better to soar over the dramatic Kenyan landscape on your approach to Loiyangalani Airport to appreciate the unique geography of the area and the striking jade green waters of the lake – the colour comes from algae.

Lake Turkana is the largest permanent desert lake in the world and the saltiest of Africa's Great Lakes. It also lies within the fossil-filled Turkana Basin, with its fascinating volcanic rock formations, which are often described as 'moonscapes'.

▲ The Nabiyotum crater is the remains of a collapsed volcano at the southern tip of Lake Turkana.

Lake Turkana Wind Power project

When the wind power project on the eastern shores of Lake Turkana is completed in 2017, it will be the biggest wind farm in Africa. The station is expected to generate 300MW of energy, which is about 20 per cent of Kenya's rising energy needs.

Birthplace of humanity

You will have to brave scorching heat to visit parts of the Turkana Basin but it's worth it to see the abundant ancient remains of dinosaurs (see right), plant life and wildlife. The region is also known as 'the cradle of humanity' because of the discovery of many human and pre-human fossils. These fossils have given experts a valuable insight into the evolution of humankind. One of the most important finds was that of a near-complete skeleton of a hominid boy, dating from about 1.5 to 1.6 million years ago.

▲ Traditional Kenyan huts are made of wood and mud, and thatched with grasses.

Traditional living

The Turkana Basin has unlocked several secrets of the past, but it is also a great place to see how the local people live now. Tribes in the area include the Turkana, whose traditional dress is woven wraps and animal skins. They raise and live mostly off livestock, such as camels. Other tribes include the Rendille, with their remarkable colourful beads, and the Gabbra.

Unfortunately, this is one of the poorest areas in Kenya and many people live in poverty. The salty water in the lake is undrinkable, so drinking water is a valuable resource. In 2013, massive groundwater reserves were discovered under the lake. If these can be extracted and supplied to the local people then their lives will change dramatically.

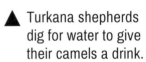

▲ Turkana shepherds dig for water to give their camels a drink.

◄ A Rendille woman wearing traditional, colourful beads.

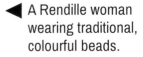

21

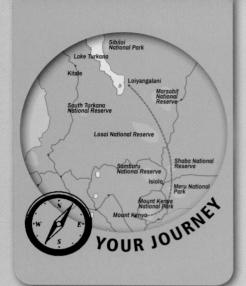

MOUNT KENYA

It's time to leave our ancient ancestors and the tribes of Lake Turkana and embark on the next leg of your journey – to Mount Kenya. Again, private plane is the fastest option, unless you fancy a long road trip. Before you get to Mount Kenya, stop off at the Shaba National Reserve, just north of the mountain, to pay homage to a pair of the world's most famous conservationists.

Born Free

The Shaba National Reserve is known for its abundant wildlife and was home to the conservationists Joy and George Adamson. Joy and George were famous for caring for Kenya's big cats. They are most famous for raising an orphaned lioness (whom they called Elsa), teaching her how to hunt and eventually returning her to the wild. Their story was made world famous by the film *Born Free*, based on Joy's book of the same name. Sadly, both George and Joy were murdered in totally unrelated incidents: George by poachers, and Joy by one of her employees.

▼ Joy Adamson and Elsa the lioness snuggle up!

Mount Kenya

Mount Kenya is the second highest mountain in Africa after Mount Kilimanjaro in Tanzania. Mount Kenya is an ancient extinct volcano (unlike Kilimanjaro, which is a dormant volcano). It is possible that it was once higher than Kilimanjaro, but over time it has been eroded by the many glaciers (frozen rivers) that flow from the peak. As the glaciers melt they form rivers that provide a major source of water for much of the local area.

▼ Mount Kenya is 5,199 m high. The country of Kenya is named after the mountain.

Climb to the top

As long as you are reasonably fit, you can attempt to walk one of the routes up Mount Kenya. There are plenty of tour companies that organise 5- or 7-day trips. They will pick you up from your accommodation and guide you up one of the three main routes to just below the snow-capped peak. Food and accommodation are provided each day. Take your time to acclimatise yourself to the altitude and take plenty of layers, as the temperature drops as you ascend into the alpine zone at around 3,000 m. Along the way you'll see amazing wildlife and beautiful views. On a clear day you might even be able to spot Mount Kilimanjaro, which lies 320 km away!

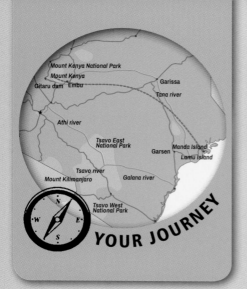

YOUR JOURNEY

MOUNT KENYA TO MANDA ISLAND

It's over 400 km from Mount Kenya National Park to your next destination, the marram grass airstrip at Manda Island. If you board a private plane you'll get an aerial view of some of Kenya's lush farmland and the Tana river – the longest river in Kenya – during your flight.

Agriculture in Kenya

The World Bank states that Kenya is one of the fastest growing economies in Africa and the agriculture sector remains its biggest earner. Some of the main cash crops include tea, coffee, beans, potatoes, cotton, tobacco and cut flowers. The area surrounding Mount Kenya and its slopes is one of the main centres for agriculture in the country.

▼ Tea pickers pluck the tea leaves by hand.

Cash crops in a cup

Rainfall and good soil is the key to agricultural success. On average it rains 200 days a year in the Mount Kenya region and the volcanic soil is very fertile. Tea and coffee grow well here because the weather is sunny but not too hot. Kenya's first tea plants were cultivated in 1903. Since then tea has become its top export crop, and Kenya is the third-largest tea exporter in the world. It specialises in black tea, the type that goes into the everyday tea bag. Coffee was introduced to Kenya around the beginning of the 20th century and is another important cash crop for Kenyan farmers.

▲ Bananas for sale at a Kenyan market.

Going bananas

Irrigation and new improved roads are other reasons why farming is thriving around Mount Kenya. Farmers have been able to grow enough crops to sell, rather than just eke out a subsistence living. In recent years, because of good irrigation, small farmers who once cultivated coffee are growing bananas instead. Bananas are an excellent and nutritious food for their families and they can make money from them as well.

Hydroelectric power supply

The Tana river is about 1,000 km long and, as you fly over it, you may be able to spot the Gitaru Dam and power station. This is Kenya's biggest hydroelectric power station. Hydroelectric power is the main generator of electricity in Kenya, but it isn't a reliable source of energy as Kenya can experience drought. The Kenyan government is currently investing money in more solar power farms and wind farms (see page 20).

▼ The Tana river winds through lush, green farmland.

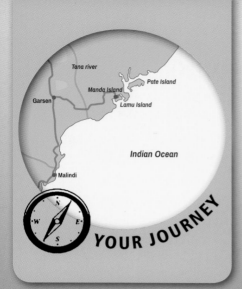

LAMU ISLAND AND BEYOND

From Manda airstrip your next stop is the beautiful island of Lamu in the Indian Ocean. Catch a ferry or hire a speedboat from the jetty close to the airstrip for the short hop to the busy port that serves this tropical island.

Lamu archipelago

Lamu Island is actually just one of the islands that make up this archipelago; the islands of Pate, Manda, Manda Toto, and Kiwayu are other tropical paradises. Lamu Island has unspoilt sandy beaches where you can swim in cobalt blue waters and explore the coral reefs. Many visitors take a trip on a sailing boat called a *dhow*. If you're lucky you'll see dolphins or sea turtles.

You should take time to stop off at least one of the other islands. The Kiwayu islanders will give you a particularly warm welcome, as fewer tourists visit this island. They will happily show you their beautiful, untouched sandy beaches, some of which have thousands of pink crabs scuttling along the shoreline.

▼ A dhow moored on the clear blue waters off Lamu Island.

Turtles in danger

The sea turtles that live off the coast of Lamu are endangered, possibly on the verge of extinction. One of the biggest problems is poachers. Turtle meat is much savoured and turtle eggs can get a good price on the black market. Construction of a deep sea commercial port at Lamu is another great threat to the turtles and if plans to build an oil pipeline under the sea and an oil refinery go ahead, then this beautiful part of the world will be changed forever.

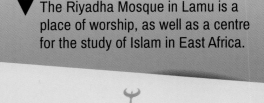

▲ A sea turtle

Lamu Old Town

Lamu Old Town has a history that goes back over 700 years. This is probably the oldest existing Swahili settlement in East Africa. It began as an ancient trading post and a centre for the slave trade. Today you can really feel the past as you walk amongst the labyrinth of narrow streets, admiring beautiful buildings with ornate doors and decoration carved from mangrove timber and coral. The people of Lamu are mostly Muslim, so look out for the Riyadha Mosque with its Islamic architecture. The town is so precious, it was made into a UNESCO World Heritage Site in 2009.

▼ The Riyadha Mosque in Lamu is a place of worship, as well as a centre for the study of Islam in East Africa.

▼ Donkeys are the main mode of transport in Lamu – watch out for donkey poo!

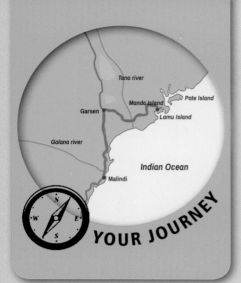

MALINDI

You've nearly reached the end of your journey around Kenya. You'll be able to take the local bus service to your final destination, Malindi. It's only 125 km from Lamu and the road has been much improved in recent years.

Marine national parks

You can swim in waters with a pleasant temperature of between 20 to 30 degrees Celsius off the coast of Malindi. If that isn't enough to tempt you into the sea then the stunning array of marine life will do the job. Malindi Marine National Reserve is actually two parks in one, as it also contains the spectacular Watamu Marine Park.

At Watamu, the coral is a couple of hundred metres from the shore and the water is crystal clear. If you go diving or snorkelling, you may see sailfish, marlin, swordfish, kingfish, lionfish, barracuda, tuna, sea turtles and octopus. If you're feeling lazy then you can always take a trip in a glass-bottomed boat!

▲ A beautiful lionfish swims among the coral.

► Local buses are a great way to travel to Malindi.

Security issues

Kenya has been in the news in recent years for terrorist attacks involving tourists. It's important to check out official travel information before travelling to any part of Kenya. Don't be surprised to see armed guards on board your bus. They are there to protect you in the unlikely event that the bus is hijacked by Somali bandits or in the event of any other danger.

Mystery of Gede

From Watamu, hire a tuk tuk to take you to the village of Gede. Hidden away in the forest are the intriguing ruins of a Swahili village, which was founded in the 12th century. These ruins include a palace, mosques and houses.

Archaeologists have found evidence to suggest the people who lived here all those years ago were highly sophisticated, and had developed their own ways of keeping food cool. Remnants of Chinese pottery and other objects show they traded overseas and were a wealthy society. Experts are today trying to unravel the mystery of why the town was abandoned in the 17th century and why there are no records of it having ever existed.

▲ The mysterious ruins of Gede.

▼ Sandstone is a sedimentary rock, made by layers of sand being deposited on top of each other over millions of years.

Heaven to hell ... and back again

About another 30 km to the north of Malindi is 'Hell's Kitchen', otherwise called the Marafa Depression (see right). The sandstone canyon has been eroded by wind, rain and flooding over the centuries. The canyon gets its name from the high temperatures recorded here – it often hits 50 degrees Celsius – and its fiery unforgiving landscape. This is the perfect place to watch your final African sunset. As the Sun goes down it lights up the different colours of the sandstone and the beauty of the jagged gorges. Get your camera out or just sit back and relax as you enjoy yet another heavenly natural wonder of Kenya.

29

GLOSSARY

4x4
Short for four-wheel-drive. A vehicle where power is supplied to all four wheels, rather than just two.

abundant
Available in large amounts.

acclimatise
To become used to a new climate or conditions.

algae
A simple type of plant with no roots or leaves.

alkaline
A substance with a pH greater than 7; the opposite of an acid.

alpine
A habitat found high up on mountains.

altitude
How high up something is.

ancient
Very old; usually refers to the time before written historical records.

arboretum
A garden planted with trees.

archaeologist
Someone who examines ancient sites and artefacts to learn about the past.

archipelago
A large group of islands.

climate
The usual weather conditions in an area over a long period of time.

cobalt
A deep, blue colour.

colonist
Someone who settles in a foreign land.

conservationist
Someone who tries to protect the environment and/or the wildlife that live in it.

creek
A narrow, sheltered waterway, such as an inlet or a channel.

cultivate
To prepare and use land for growing crops.

dormant
Temporarily inactive.

Equator
An imaginary line around the middle of Earth, an equal distance from the North and South Poles.

erode
To gradually wear away over time.

extinction
When a species completely dies out.

fault
A break in a rock formation.

fertile
Able to produce lots of vegetation.

fusion cuisine
Food created using a mixture of styles, often from different cultures.

glacier
A slow-moving river of ice formed from compacted mountain snow.

gorge
A narrow valley between steep, rocky cliffs.

hominid
A term that refers to all the great apes (including humans) and their ancestors.

hospitality
Friendliness towards friends and strangers.

hydroelectric power
Electricity generated by the movement of water.

irrigation
When water is moved from canals and rivers to drier areas to help with growing crops.

labyrinth
A maze.

marram grass
A coarse grass that grows on sandy coasts and sand dunes.

parasite
Something that lives and feeds off another living thing. Fleas are parasites.

poacher
A person who illegally hunts animals, often for money.

protectorate
A country that is protected and controlled by another.

repellent
A substance that stops insects from biting.

seizure
A sudden illness, such as a fit.

semi-nomadic
People who generally move around the countryside, but keep a base camp to return to.

settler
Someone who moves to an area and stays there for a long time.

soda lake
A body of water containing a lot of salts.

subsistence farmer
A farmer who grows enough food to feed their family, but not enough to sell.

tectonic plates
The separate plates that make up the Earth's crust and slowly change position over long periods of time.

tropical
The hot, wet areas just above and below the Equator.

BOOKS TO READ

Non-fiction

A Child's Day in: My Life in Kenya by Alex Woolf (Franklin Watts, 2015)

Animals of the Masai Mara by Adam Scott Kennedy (WILDGuides, 2012)

Countries in Our World: Kenya by Alison Brownlie Bojang (Franklin Watts, 2013)

DK Eyewitness Travel Guide: Kenya by Phillip Briggs and Lizzie Williams (Dorling Kindersley, 2015)

Kenya Travel Maps International Adventure Map by National Geographic Maps (2012)

Lonely Planet: Kenya Travel Guide by Anthony Ham (Lonely Planet, 2015)

The Rough Guide to Kenya by Philip Trillo (Rough Guides, 2013)

Fiction

Born Free by Joy Adamson (Pan, re-issued 2010)

The Butterfly Lion by Michael Morpurgo (HarperCollins Children's Books, 1996)

WEBSITES

The UK government gives important advice about travel to Kenya on its website. Check here for up-to-date information about the areas to avoid (terrorism is a major concern), visas and health.
https://www.gov.uk/foreign-travel-advice/kenya

Rough Guides present great information about travel to countries all around the world. The Kenyan guide features the places not to miss, sites and cities to explore, safaris to savour and suggested itineraries, as well as inspirational galleries of photographs to whet your appetite for travel.
www.roughguides.com/destinations/africa/kenya/

Lonely Planet presents a fantastic array of things to do in Kenya, plus in-depth information about the cities of Nairobi and Mombasa. This is a must for any young traveller who wants to be inspired and well-informed about their adventures in Kenya.
www.lonelyplanet.com/kenya

Magical Kenya is the official website for the Kenya Tourism Board. There is plenty to explore on this site, including where to visit and what to see, as well as the latest news about travel in Kenya.
http://www.magicalkenya.com

The National Geographic website for kids provides fast facts at your fingertips about Kenya. Zip to this site for bites of information about the geography, nature, culture, government and history of Kenya.
http://www.ngkids.co.uk/places/country-fact-file-kenya

Note to parents and teachers:
Every effort has been made by the Publishers to ensure that the websites in this book are suitable for children, that they are of the highest educational value, and that they contain no inappropriate or offensive material. However, because of the nature of the Internet, it is impossible to guarantee that the contents of these sites will not be altered. We strongly advise that Internet access is supervised by a responsible adult.

INDEX